Life of a Recovering

(Parts of this story appeared in a small magazine that contains stories of people in alcoholic recovery. The magazine receives between 100 and 200 entries a month. How fortunate I feel this story was picked. It was printed in French, Spanish and English, being sent to recovery groups all over the world.)

I was born in Ironwood, MI on June 26, 1927. My parents worked for my grandfather who had a lumber camp. I also had a brother who was 3 years older than I. We were raised at the camp, located between Mercer and Hurley, WI until I was 3 years old. Oh the stories my mother would tell about the lumber camp and how she not only took care of us but feeding six hungry lumber jacks plus seven of my father's family. Or how the bunk house smelled most of the time, especially when the 'jacks were drying out their wool socks by the pot-bellied stove…"Whew"! They didn't have showers or baths; all they had was a sauna and a small creek that ran through the camp.

These same hard working men also drank as hard on their trips into Hurley. Once they got paid, off they'd go up to Hurley, usually using a "dray" or a large sled and a team of horses. Imagine a bunch of men headed to town, 15 miles away, in the middle of winter. That was a ten hour trip for my father to make. Head up to town, drag their butts out of jail for drinkin' and a fightin'. Then again, Hurley, in its heyday was only four blocks long and had over forty taverns. Of course the men would buy clothes first, before they ended up in jail or possibly broke. However, some of them would give us not just packages of gum and candy, but whole boxes of that stuff! And, not only that, some would hand us money and that meant we actually had bank accounts when we left the lumber camp.

Grandfather was a hard man to work for and was harder on my father. When my father had had enough abuse, he used a trip up to town to sell a horse for my grandfather and after getting $75 for it, headed up to Duluth, MN where he shipped out on the ore boats.

Let me share with you some stuff about our family's origin. My mother's parents came from Finland and wound up living on a farm and had a total of five girls and three boys. With four of the children still living at home, they had gone into town and came back to a house that no longer existed; it had burned down and all the money they had went up with it because grandfather didn't believe in banks. They lost everything. At the present time, only two of my mother's sisters are alive: Fay, who lives in Waukesha, and Judy who lives in Ironwood, MI. Judy and I get together often for lunch. I really admire her for her determination in life. My mother was a beautiful, loving, and caring person and my father was kind and generous - until he drank, then he became a different person.

When I was nine years old we moved to different neighborhoods, where I attended four different grade schools. It wasn't fun always moving. Part of the reason, is my older brother was not strong and very thin. I defended my brother so much that it was known throughout the neighborhood that if you wanted to get me mad, pick on my brother. One time, after my brother had died at the age of thirteen, the neighborhood bully said, "I bet you're glad that your brother died so you could have his bicycle." I asked another boy for his gloves and pounded the snot out of that bully. Saying that to me really hurt. I was devastated when my brother died. He had been driven to one of my aunt's home and died there. I still remember how I felt, nearly 80 years later.

Lake Gogebic – what a place to live your summers as a kid. The lake was about 17 miles long and a couple of miles wide. I have many fond memories of those summers, fishing with family and the sound of the rain on the shingled roof, the waves washing up on shore. I believe I was about 7 and until around age 14 that our family would bring an older lady, who owned the cottage, out to the lake every summer and we would stay with her. She had a springer spaniel named Buddy. He would rock himself to sleep on the porch swing until we heard a thump. My brother and I would look at each other and exclaim, "I guess Buddy fell asleep."

One of my memories is staying on the dock as our parents went out on the lake fishing. We were inside playing around when Buddy started barking. So, my brother and I went outside to check it out. Oh my gosh, one of the cane poles was really bent over with a fish on it. Well, I set the hook and yanked him out of the water. It wasn't bass season yet, so we hid the fish under the cottage. We found out later it was a four pound four ounce perch. Later that week, my dad went into town and spoke to the local sports dealer about the fish. When he looked it up, we had a record fish. He then asked, "Where is it?" My dad replied that we ate it....so much for the record perch.

My dad was of the belief that the rougher the weather the better the fishing because it would stir up the fish. One of those "rough times" we were on the lake and the neighbor was headed in and shouted to his friend, "There go those crazy fishermen, the Fin Landers!" At that very moment, my brother and I were bailing out the boat with a coffee can and a minnow bucket. Dad would either try to row, or if he got tired my mother would row with one oar and I and my brother would pull on the other oar. Fun!

Back then there weren't any refrigerators and there was no electricity to the cottage; however, we did have an ice house. These were buildings with blocks of ice covered in saw dust, that we kept our fish and dairy products in. This was during the depression years and I'm not sure if there was even tin foil yet. We ate a lot of fish and wild game. Mom had a unique way of baking the fish: she would roll them up in newspaper, wet the paper and put it on the red, hot coals in the wood stove. The paper would get black, thin and brittle yet, when you would open the paper, great baked white fish would appear!

High School

Booze. My problems began in high school. One of my friend's fathers owned a wholesale bakery company. There was a tavern next door and his father set it up so that his son could pick up beer for the bakers. Well, we four friends were the bakers: drinking quarts of beer in the back of a panel truck! No matter when we drank, I drank the most and I never knew why, or did I?

I had my first blackout on prom night. I had bought a fifth of bourbon and we headed to a cottage party where the girls wouldn't let us drink. So, I took it upon myself to try to drink the whole bottle. They stuck my head in the lake and drove me home where they stuck me between the doors, rang the doorbell and ran away. My mother opened the door where I fell into the house and she asked, "What happened?" I meant to say, "Someone spiked my drink", but instead I foolishly blurted out, "Someone spiked my chickens!" My mother,

God bless her, remembered that instance until she got Alzheimer's and passed away. As later in the story will reveal, I had thankfully gotten sober before she passed away.

When I was sixteen, or the summer of 1943, I was hired as a chore boy for Notre Dame Estate, owned by Martin Gillen. When he died, the estate was willed to Notre Dame. The property contained 9,000 acres and had 19 private lakes. It was located near Land O' Lakes, WI and had a large summer house and a winter house on one of the lakes. There was also a boathouse with an apartment, which is where I stayed. Mr. Gillen had his own gas pump and road equipment along with some garages that had an antique 1928 Cadillac, 1930 Duesenberg and a couple of other cars I can't recall.

Anyhow, my job was to take Mr. Gillen fishing and to drive him into Ironwood, MI on business. I also needed to pick up the priests that would come and visit the property. I would pick them up from the train station in Minocqua and would drive everyone around the property and lakes.

At the time I was hired, my dad had been out of work, so he and my mother were also hired on. It didn't last long. One day, my father was across one of the lakes working with the caretaker when the siren went off. Thinking that I had drowned or that my mother had had a heart attack, he sped across the lake, ran inside to Mr. Gillen and asked what happened. Now, the siren was for emergency situations only, but Mr. Gillen told my dad that he wanted to check up on what they were doing. My dad told him that he quit, right there on the spot. Thank goodness it didn't affect my relationship with Mr. Gillen.

One day when Mr. Gillen was fishing from the road he happened to get his fishing lure stuck out in the deep, cold running water by some culverts. He told me to go in and fetch his lure; I refused! He sternly told me to get in the back of the car and I thought, well, there goes my job. Mr. Gillen, however, went to my mother and told her, "That son of yours! I love that independent little S.O.B.!" I was the only employee that was invited to have dinner with him.

On one of our trips into town, he had some business to attend to and said it would be awhile, and I should go see my parents. On the way to see them, I knew some of my pals were working at a local sawmill. Well, of course I had to stop by and show off this great big limo I was driving! Only 16 years old and here I was driving a limo. Boy, did that feel great!

I also had a couple of occasions that, looking back now, were possible tests of my honesty. One time there was a large roll of money that had been left on the edge of the cushion. I returned it and he just smiled. On another occasion, I told him there was a flat tire on the limo and I knew how to change the tire. He told me when I was done to bring the nail to him. When I did, he said the nail looks a little odd. I told him, "I guess that's because I pounded it into the tire so I could prove to you that I could change a tire!" There are more stories of that summer at the Estates, however, I'll save that for another time.

When I was ready to head back to school, Mr. Gillen gave me a Buick Club Coupe to use so I would have transportation to come and visit on the weekends. Before I left, he had put several frozen chickens in the car to give to my folks. Mr. Gillen died three weeks after I went back to school. I understand there were thoughts of him putting me in his will for funds for a college education. Just prior to me leaving, Mr. Gillen told me, with the cook as a witness, in case anything happened to him, he was giving me a key to the gate so I could come back to fish or hunt anytime. I did this a couple of times with a pal and then the priests changed the locks. I never went back.

Service Time

I graduated from high school in 1945. The Navy let us graduate early, probably about fifteen of us boys, and then report for duty a few days later. There were three of us that would spend time together: Chris, Leon and myself. We volunteered for the Navy Seabees after a month of Navy training. After the training, we had a week of liberty, so we headed home before reporting for Marine basic in California. While home on liberty, I told my buddies that I always had a goal; to have one shot of whiskey in every tavern in Hurley, WI. Back in 1945, the population of Hurley was about 5,000 and the main drag of about 6 blocks and nearby streets had roughly

70 taverns. It ended up being called the "Death March" because trying to accomplish this task **was** a death march. I had a friend follow us to count the taverns we visited and made it through twenty six before I ended up sleeping under the bushes at my parents' house. Then it was off to California for training.

My two friends ended up with different draft numbers for overseas. Their number came up and we said our goodbyes and "see ya at home"; had we only known then we would cross paths a couple of times while serving in the South Seas. A few weeks later my number was called. We were issued fur-lined boots and parkas. We thought we were headed for the Aleutian Islands; instead, we found ourselves sitting in Tokyo Bay for ten days. While sitting and waiting for our next assignment, I found out the boat next to ours was a Seabees boat and the number was C.D. 7, the same number my buddies had drawn back in California. Macarthur didn't want Seabees on Japan after sitting in the bay for ten days, so I first watched as my buddies shipped out, not knowing where they were headed and a few days later we were on our way to Guam.

I will never forget the humidity and heat when I got off the barge. Then, lo and behold, the first morning at the chow line, I spotted Chris and Leon. Now, during our time on Guam, there were a few "humorous" events, of course. One of which was putting on a camp show by wearing coconut halves for our busts and mop heads for our hair and doing some hula dance to Hawaiian music. I was, from that point forward, nicknamed "swivel hips." (Later, when I was out of the service and went home, I was at the track and bet on a horse named "Swivel Hips" who hadn't won in three years. Still, I bet on him at thirty to one odds for two dollars: that horse went on to win and I won ninety-six dollars!)

Back on Guam, hard liquor was hard to find, only near beer, but I did manage to buy several pints of rum from an officer for a high price. That, was my second blackout. Not long after that, my friends were shipped off to Saipan and three weeks later I also headed to Saipan in a storm, but we toughed it out and made it during the middle of the night. And to my surprise, I was sleeping two bunks away from Chris, and Leon was a few hundred yards away!

While on Saipan there were, again, a few incidents I'd like to share. One happened while I was drunk and wanted to know if a jeep could float, so I drove it into the ocean. Nope, only bubbles surfaced and that was that. Another time, while working in a coral pit, I had six Japanese prisoners and one of them had been a lawyer in Tokyo who didn't want to go to war. He spoke English because he had attended college in the United States. His name was Takahashi Yoshina. He became a trustee, an interpreter; he was important to the Japanese army because he knew English. This one particular time, after using the latrine, Takahashi came back to me and said, "Bobby, you forgot something." He handed me my side arm that was a fully loaded .45.

The temperature in the coral pit would average 110 degrees with the sun shining on the white coral. When we needed time off, although it wasn't right, I would throw a crow bar into the rock crusher and the belt would break. They needed to send another belt from Guam, which meant time off for us. We were part of a blasting crew and for fun, one time, when we were all loaded up in the dump box of the truck, I started to move and then pull the lever, tipping the box of my truck. The prisoners would be hanging on by their fingertips and yelling loudly in Japanese. I then lowered the box and yelled, "Who is number one?" They quickly replied, "Bobby Ichy Bon." After that, anytime I asked them who is number one, they would reply, "Bobby Ichy Bon."

Speaking of our blasting crew, sometimes they would use too much explosives and the rocks would hit the roofs of the Navy Quonset huts down the road. On one particular occasion, we were not informed that another crew was going to blast. We were across the way, at the canvas latrines doing our business when we heard the blast and the ground shook. My pals asked, "What are we going to do?" I replied, "Pray!" Just then, large rocks fell all around us, some even coming through the latrine. Although no one got hurt, I had to chuckle to myself and think had I been killed what the local paper headline would read…"Local man killed by big rock while sitting in a canvas latrine."

When we were being shipped out to head back to the states, the Bikini Atom bomb was detonated. Ships radios said this would cause a tidal wave that would destroy everything within a hundred miles. When they announced the bomb's release, we all gathered at the ship's rail and watched in that direction wondering if something was going to happen. It didn't, thankfully.

Work

When the three of us got back stateside, Chris stayed in the area, as did I. In fact, I got married and Leon moved to Lansing, MI and got married. When he was twenty four years old, his wife shot him twice then killed herself. She fell against an oil stove and part of her face was burned off. Sadly, at the funeral, there were two hearses going down the main street of our small town.

Chris ended up moving to Milwaukee, WI where he worked for General Motors as a supervisor. He would be involved in making the moon buggy and lived with the astronauts for two weeks in California. When their mission was done on the moon they left behind a container with a list of names involved in constructing the moon buggy. So if you ever get to the moon, look for that container, my friend Chris's name is on it.

When I returned home after trying my hand at college, I was involved in a bad car accident, breaking my back. This accident actually happened in front of the office of a sawmill I was supposed to work for the next day. The vehicle slid on some ice and hit a telephone pole in front of the office; how's that for ironic? That job never came to be because I ended up in a body cast from under my armpits to my waist. This happened in November 1946. The cast came off in March and I actually shipped out on the ore boats in May as a coal passer and then promoted to fireman. Now, this was hard work. You were expected to shovel a ton and a half of coal every hour: four hours on, eight hours off. On your time off the galley was open twenty-four hours a day and you could help yourself to all the food you could eat. Figuratively, it **was** back-breaking work and I couldn't finish out the season because of my back. I was surprised I lasted as long as I did considering my injury.

After the ore boat job I headed to Pontiac, MI and worked on an assembly line for two companies - General Motors and Pontiac Motors. Well, neither of these were for me. It was then that I heard from a buddy of mine working at a country club in Glenview, IL.

Getting Hooked on Golf and Alcohol

My buddy was working at the country club and told me there was an opening for me as a bus boy with a chance of moving up to a better job. I did move up to what they termed a houseman and headwaiter. I wore a white uniform with an Eisenhower jacket and black bow tie. I was the only waiter to serve drinks in the main dining room. During dance night, I would assign different tables to different waiters; keeping the best tipping tables to myself of course! I also worked the Keno nights and brought the money to the winners. On occasion, I would tend bar at members' homes. After all, this was a very wealthy membership and a beautiful country club; it was rated one of the top ten in the region.

I became hooked on the game of golf and more so on alcohol. Part of the reason is, quite frankly, I didn't have to pay for my drinks. Also, dates were readily available because the waitresses stayed right at the club. One episode that sticks in my mind is getting so drunk that I passed out in the backseat of one of the caddy buses parked right next to my upstairs room of the caddy shack. Evidently, I couldn't make it to my room. This young caddy finds me and yells,

"I think he's dead" and another caddy says, "I saw him breathing." This was one of many blackouts I was going to drink myself to over the next few years.

I knew I didn't want to continue this line of work, even with the great tips and available companionship. We put in long hours, many times 14 to 16 hour shifts. So I went to downtown Chicago and took a career aptitude test that took many hours to complete. During the interview afterwards, it became quite clear that I should do something in sales. It took eight years for that to happen. Anyhow, I went back to work and one of the members asked if I would like to work for him and learn the retail lumber business. A a friend of his asked me to come work for him and learn the insurance business. I was more interested in the lumber business.

I was twenty two years old at the time that I went to work for him at fifty dollars a week. He put me through the paces: unloading box cars full of lumber throughout the good part of winter, relieving the switchboard girl, the order desk, making out the payroll and waiting on customers. His plan was to have me available to fill in wherever and whenever needed. That didn't pan out, however, because the yard manager ended up having a nervous breakdown. There I was at twenty two years old; the youngest yard manager in the Chicago area with fifteen yard people and six truck drivers, not to mention having to hire more laborers when multiple boxcars came in to be unloaded, plus outside tractor and trailers to supplement the six we had.

I will tell you this, it wasn't too far down the road until the drinking caught up to me. I didn't know the city, which I needed to learn, and I had to make out between 50 and 100 invoices a day. The stress started to mount. I would go to the local tavern with the men at the ten o'clock break and at three p.m., with stops along the way home. I drank….a lot!

One time at Christmas, after drinking with the guys, I was in a car accident. I had blacked out and rear-ended a car. Imagine my shock when the man from the car accident called me at work and said he didn't want the police involved because they would probably lock me up. He knew I had been drinking. I left the company soon after that on good terms. The owner was planning on going out of business. My boss got a job for me at a cooperative wholesale supply company that he was an officer of in Franklin Park, IL.

By this time I was a married man and we had two daughters. When this new opportunity came about, my wife wanted to move back up north. She did move, hoping I would follow and get a job up there. I didn't, and while we were apart my drinking increased. Here's how it went: the night before I headed for an interview in Juliet, IL I got drunk, blind drunk. I was in bad shape when I hit the road in the morning. Although I wanted an eye-opener, I didn't. When I arrived at the company, the man and I talked for a little while and then he handed me an application. I told him I'd send it back after I filled it out. No, he wanted me to fill it out in front of him. He knew something was wrong as he watched me, as I shakily tried to fill it out. So, he said, "I don't know what your problem is young man, but why don't we just forget about this." How humiliating, but I did land the job. My first selling job opened for me in northern WI. This meant a lot of traveling and an open expense account. This, was an opportunity for more drinking.

Family

I was married with two children by this time. Our second daughter, Mary Beth, was born but sad to say she died twenty months later. This was a very sad time in our lives. We were living in Green Bay, WI at the time. We were going to take a trip up north to our hometown, Ironwood, MI. but Mary Beth seemed to be out of sorts so we took her to see the doctor. He said that she was cutting teeth and the trip might do her some good. The second day she was crying a lot. We had our family doctor make a house call and he said she had an infected ear and gave us a prescription. The following day I picked Mary Beth up out of her crib and she was pulling her hair. I looked at her eyes and I could see her pupils were dilated. I knew she was in trouble. We took her to the emergency room at the local hospital. The doctor said she had Emphaseinas; infection of the brain after a case of the measles. She started choking and the machine that kept the airway clear of phlegm stopped working. I frantically ran down the hallways screaming for help. It was only moments later that she died. A minister came to console me and I told him, "Don't talk to me about God!" I would find my faith later in my life.

We returned to Green Bay and the doctor's office called and told us that Mary Beth was past due for her appointment. I told the secretary she had passed away. A short time later the doctor was at our door. He was crying, and I understood why. He was a new, young doctor and this was the first patient he lost, and it turned out to be a child. To this day, I cannot put into words how heartsick I was over our loss.

It was eight weeks later that we received a call from the Ironwood health department. We were advised that Mary Beth died from spinal T.B. My wife, daughter Marcia and I had to go get x-rays to see if we had it. When we got the call, it was only I who had T.B. and was told they needed me to go straight to the sanitarium. I asked the doctor "for how long" and he said it could be three years! I had just finished a round of golf and was feeling in good health. Heck, I didn't even have a cough.

While I was in the sanitarium, I felt like I had picked up the T.B. germ on the road and given it to my daughter. I felt responsible for her death. I told one of the nurses about this and she said, "Come with me please. I want to show you something." On the second floor, where the children and mothers were, there on a bed was a five year old American Indian girl, with her sad mother, unable to speak or respond to anything. She had been in a coma from T.B. and survived. In that moment, my faith was restored to me.

After eight weeks in the sanitarium my tests came back negative, even after I had been told that I originally had T.B. Anyhow, I was able to go home one weekend a month. While I was in the sanitarium I found ways to drink…..and get drunk. After one Christmas visit, I was listening to Christmas music on the way back to the sanitarium and I thought, "To hell with it" and I stopped off at a bar and got drunk. I also bought a bottle to take back to the sanitarium. That night they brought my dinner to the room and I passed out with my face in the mashed potatoes.

I was fortunate that the three year sentence was whittled down to six months. However, I gained twenty pounds in those six months. The women patients had made me a diploma that was put in a frame that one of them had made. It said I was a walking example of a person that got so well, even though he broke all the rules. So, I arranged for a pizza and beer party. I managed to get a pizza place to deliver it the seven miles to the sanitarium.

On the darker side of being diagnosed with T.B. was the stigma attached to it. No one would come visit you, the neighborhood kids were told not to play with our daughter and the kids avoided her in school because they might catch it.

Drinkin', Jobs and Family

When we lived in Green Bay, WI we could walk to Lambeau Field and actually hear Lombardi shouting at his players on the practice field. Come to think of it, those players: Jim Taylor, Ron Kraemer, Ray Nitschke and others all lived within a few blocks of us. In fact, my daughter went to school with Bart Starr's son.

The company I worked for provided me with tickets to Packer games to take prospective clients and customers after entertaining them at our home. In 1958 the Packers had two wins and ten losses. Then Lombardi took over and they entered their glory years. The company was great to work for. They had allowed me to take a company car home on my visits when I was in the sanitarium, they paid me a salary all the while I was in there, and of course, the chance to entertain clients at Packer games. During this time, I continued to drink more; not every day, but I would binge drink. I wouldn't drink for months and then I would go on a binge. For a year after our daughter's death, I wound up in detox twice; that still didn't stop me.

Two years after Mary Beth's death, we had a third daughter named Greta. However, my marriage was falling apart. We found out after getting married that we weren't compatible. To give you an example, when Marcia was five, she said, "Daddy, why doesn't mommy like you?" Two other examples - my wife telling me that she didn't need affection and if I found someone during my road trips to go ahead, it would be ok with her; and the minister who used me as a subject in one of his sermons. He said it's terrible to find a man that's both father and mother to his children and still a stranger in his own home. Now, I will admit that my drinking didn't help our marriage, but I'm not self-justifying it either, for our compatibility wasn't there from the start. Even our minister, who said he would never advise any of his congregation to separate from their spouse, advised me to keep a receipt of the money I sent to the family. I left Green Bay in 1965.

I headed back south to Chicago and the lumber business. I was heartsick leaving my daughters. I got a job behind the counter of a retail lumber company due to my past experience. About six months in, I went on a four day binge and got fired. I went back home to Ironwood and lived with my parents for a while, then I called the company and they were willing to hire me back. This time, it was a few months in and I went on another binge and was fired...again. This should have been my rock bottom; after all, I was living in an old hotel with a bunch of drunks. I had a friend pick me up and put me on a train for Ironwood.

After a month, I decided to go to Milwaukee because I had an uncle and aunt living there. I didn't think I could find a job in the lumber business so I got a job in a company making pool tables. I was fired from there for drinking. It was on that binge that a hometown buddy of mine brought me to detox. While I was in the detox center, my Dad called me up and said that the saw mill he was working at had an opening for a salesman and he would have the owner give me a call. If he only knew that he was talking to me in a detox facility.

The owner of the saw mill told me he would furnish me with a car and a full expense account. I asked him what the pay would be and he told me. I told him I was looking for a higher wage than he had to offer. Imagine the arrogance! Lo and behold, I got the higher wage. I went to work for him and lasted one year. Then, I went on another binge and wound up in detox.

When I got out of detox the following weekend, I called a local wholesale lumber company. I told them about leaving the previous employer because there was a personality conflict. Then I thought for a minute. And I said to hell with it, I'm not going to lie to get the job. I told him I just got out of detox. He appreciated my honesty. He did call some of my customers and was told I had an alcohol problem. Still, he hired me and gave me a company car and an open expense account. I asked him what he was going to pay me and I told him I was thinking about something higher. He said "let's see what you can do before we agree to that", and I asked when I could start. On the very first day I sold two truckloads and two car loads of lumber. It was in short order that I received a raise.

I worked for him for twenty years and was fired five times. I went to detox seven times in three different treatment centers. I was arrogant because I knew he would take me back; the other salesman wasn't able to make my accounts buy from him. Later, that salesman quit but had his son hired. His son didn't like to travel and be away from his friends.

My boss cut out my bonuses, so after twenty years I looked for another job. At this time, I had been completely sober for five years. I was sober because I had found a group with a lot of new friends that supported me. Funny thing is, my boss was involved in fraud with my best customer. He was charging for more lumber than was being received. I called my customer after I had made copies of the incoming lumber invoices and our invoices. We put my boss out of business. I was in my sixties by this time and lost transportation because the company car was all I had. I also lost my life and health insurance and had no idea what would happen with my retirement plan. My boss was taken to court and found guilty of over one hundred cases of fraud. They had found several other customer cases as they went through all of the invoices.

I was still sober and went to work for my previous customer for five years. I stayed sober and produced well, but he wouldn't give me a telephone expense. I left that company and went to work for another local wholesale company, Corullo Lumber Co. I again stayed sober and produced well. What a wonderful man to work for. I have not been able to make any sales for more than ten years because the lumber brokerage business no longer exists. This man still pays my supplementary insurance and cell phone expenses.

While I had been working for the fraudulent employer I had a heart attack. The doctor's orders were to quit smoking and loose twenty five pounds or I would die. What bedside manners! But, it worked. I did what he told me to do.

The other very important part of my family life during this time was in 1969 when I met a wonderful, beautiful and talented lady. We met in January and got married in May. I had been dry for about a year. On our wedding night, we had a discussion that I was going to have a happy marriage and that meant we could celebrate with Champagne….and away we go! The next night it was martinis. This was May and by Christmas I was in Hazelden: a well-known treatment center. I stayed sober for a year and was off and running again. I would end up in a treatment center called Why Not. Even at this point, I couldn't accept that I had a drinking problem even after all the binges and blackouts.

Binges, Blackouts, Detox and Treatment Centers

I know how important it is to regale you all with stories of failed attempts at trying to stay sober. It's even more important that I have, after many failed attempts, stayed sober for 35 years and counting. But I would like to share a handful of excerpts of miserably failed attempts. Mainly because I was not ready to sober up, not even when I seemed to have hit the bottom a few too many times.

One time, I fell on my face while in detox and broke my upper plate in three places and consulted a dentist to see if he could do anything. He said he would try, but not give any assurances; yet, he glued it together and it lasted twenty five years! Another time I was going to commit suicide by jumping off a bridge in De Pere, WI. My salesmen friends said I couldn't even do that right, for there was only about three feet of water and I would have probably only broken my legs.

On another unmemorable day, I was on highway 29 going east towards Green Bay; back then it was only a two lane highway and it carried heavy traffic as the main highway across Wisconsin. One of my customers spotted me clearing cars and semis off the road as I was swerving across both lanes of traffic, blind drunk of course! He blew his horn, trying to get me to stop but it just made me speed up more. So he gave up. I saw him a few weeks later and he asked me how I got home. I had no idea what he was talking about. That was a major blackout.

On a particularly disturbing day, I woke up on our sofa with torn pants and the station wagon had a dent in it. I had horrible memories about killing a man in an accident in Chicago, but it didn't stop me from drinking.

Daughter's Wedding

Now, I could go on and on about countless times - some funny, some not, that I found myself blind drunk, passed out, blacked out or whatever, until an event in my life finally hit home: my daughter's wedding day. Unfortunately, or perhaps fortunately, I got blind drunk the night before our oldest daughter's wedding. The next day, even though I was craving the next drink, my daughter told me, "Dad, if you get drunk today I will not talk to you for the rest of my life." Her words continued to echo over and over in my mind. This incident is easy to remember because it was the next to my last drink and binge. I know how long she has been married because it was the last year I drank; 35 years ago…and counting!

Looking Back on Family

As I have shared earlier, I have been married twice; the first time was for seven years, during which we had three daughters (I have two granddaughters and two grandsons). The second time was for twenty three years. She lives in Sault St. Marie, MI with her first husband. We still remain good friends. We talk on the phone at least twice a week. Heck, she even gave me her car because her health won't let her drive, and every Christmas she sends me a check. How many ex-husbands can make that claim?

As for the kids, one daughter is a chemist and the other has had leadership positions with several companies. The grandkids: one granddaughter has her Doctorate in Physical Therapy and is the Director of PT at a large healthcare management company, the other granddaughter works as a successful freelance writer and loves her job, one grandson is a program manager for a child welfare organization, and the other grandson is a compliance trust specialist for an asset management company.

I value the love of and for my family. I value greatly my thirty-five years of complete and wonderful sobriety. It's not the quantity but the quality. I am also grateful that I have survived three major surgeries. But, before I go there, let's reminisce about....the past.

Thoughts of Yesteryear

I would like to take the time to share pieces of my struggles through detoxes, treatment centers, family and friends, if I may. Perhaps some of you may relate to these situations.

I checked into a small six unit motel in a small town. Later that night I met another salesman whom I had never met. We soon found out that we had something in common; we were both alcoholics. We proceeded to get drunk that night. The next morning, after checking out, I stopped by a local bar for an eye opener. Lo and behold, there was my new pal. We drank and played cribbage most of the day and in the afternoon we went down by the lake and got several hours of sleep. That night, I ended up at the same supper club. By that time, I was really out of it. I then headed across the road to the same motel but I couldn't find my key. Well, I went to the office and no one was there. I was desperate and needed a bed. Then, I remembered the room I had been in. I noticed a window was open so I tried taking the screen off to let myself in when I heard some guy yelling, "What the Hell!!" I forgot I had checked out that morning. So, I went back to the office and slept in a recliner until daybreak. Later that day I showed up drunk at my company, and yet, they gave me another chance. A person would think after all the blackouts I would realize I was an alcoholic and could not safely take a drink.

I was staying in a motel in Green Bay, WI and woke up at three a.m. and I desperately needed a drink. I looked in the toilet tank, no bottle of booze. I sat down, lit a cigarette and the lighter fell to the floor and rolled underneath the bed. Now, the maids should always clean a room thoroughly, right? Well, not this time. I found a bottle, hopefully a full bottle of booze. Wouldn't you know my luck, not only was it full but it was Christian Brothers Brandy. I was set for at least that day.

Six months later, same motel, same shape. I was again hoping that the maid slipped up, which she had. This time, I think God was trying to tell me something because under the bed was a dog turd!

I was admitted to a hospital for detox, about sixty miles from my home by a friend. After dropping me off, my friend stopped by a friend of his to chat for a bit. When he called my wife to let her know that her husband was tucked in for the night, she replied, "The heck you have, he's home." I had skipped out of the hospital and hitchhiked home with a person who was going right by my house. How fortunate for me; or was it?

A different episode that happened at the same hospital a bit later: I was given a shot that should have put me out for hours but when he checked in on me, I was awake and showed him my very shaky hand trying to take a drink of water. I told him the medication didn't help. He then asked, "Would a shot of whiskey help?" A short time later his wife walked in to see how I was doing. I knew both of them outside the hospital setting. I put on the fake shaky hands again. She said, "Didn't my husband give you anything?" I said yes, but it didn't work. She said, "Would a shot of whiskey help?" I told her it wouldn't hurt to try. She came back with a double shot. Well, I wore out my welcome and the doctor called the coordinator on alcoholism in the area. They found room for me at a treatment center in central Wisconsin called Why Not. Come to think of it, it reminds me of a year earlier that I had been in Hazelden. I'll cover that in a bit.

I was driven down to the treatment center by the coordinator, a friend of mine and my dad. The doctor had let them know that he had given me a shot that would have knocked out a horse for twelve hours. When I arrived, it looked like an old fishing lodge. I walked into the lobby and said, "Where's the bar?" They put me in intensive care with two other patients. When I was alone in the room, I was making calls on the phone and ordering martinis. When that didn't work, I stole a pair of shoes and a jacket from one of the other guys that was there. They had taken these things away from me. I hit the road. They found me a short distance away hiding in a ditch. That evening, I went out to the parking lot looking for a car with keys in the ignition. After not finding any, I found a station wagon that was open, crawled in and fell asleep on the backseat. I woke up because the vehicle was riding on a bumpy road. Let me say the woman driving was a bit surprised to see me rise up in the back of her car! She would later refer to me as "the roadrunner". Turns out, she was the head nurse at the center. Years later, she was giving a talk in a center close to my home and told the story of the roadrunner. I did leave the treatment center on good terms after thirty days.

Hazelden and Why Not

I had a previous stay at a place called Hazelden. My plan was to get out in a minimum stay of twenty one days. Needless to say, I didn't get much out of it and wound up in Why Not a year later.

While at Hazelden all of us had a job to do. My job was to pick up the dirty laundry in the women's unit. I was supposed to yell, "Man in the house." Instead, I would softly call, "Man in the house." When I got back to my unit, all the guys would ask, "What did you see this morning?" Not much happened at Hazelden, except in our unit there was a member, Father Bill, who as it turned out, would be waiting for me at Why Not as a counselor.

In my very first session with Father Bill he told the other members that he could hear Bob's thoughts, "I know Father Bill and can work him over and get out of here easily." He continued, "I have news for him, knowing me is not an asset but a liability because I know what a phony he can be!"

My job, while at Why Not, was to make the early morning coffee. They had a dog, of the boxer breed, whose name was King. King loved me. I would use round bologna lunch meat as flying saucers for King to catch. That was fun. When we would have a speaker at one of our sessions, he would lie down next to me and fall asleep. The problem was, he would snore like a lumberjack so I had to point at him so the others knew who it was. I was able to leave after my thirty day stint. It wouldn't be for another seven years that I ended up at the last detox treatment center. In that span of time, I was known as a binge drinker. I would be sober for months and then binge drink from three to six days at a stretch.

Finally, we arrive at the last detox treatment center. I was staying in a hotel/bar/restaurant sixty miles from home. I had been drinking for six days when I just about crawled into the manager's office and asked for help. He had been waiting for me; he was also a deputy sheriff. My room was littered with bottles of vodka and Maalox. Maalox was to keep the vodka down. He had one of the patrolmen drive me to detox about sixty-five miles away.

Four days after my last drink, I was slurring my words as if I was still drunk. Boy, I knew then what it means to have brain damage in alcoholics. I was taken to the hospital connected to the treatment center. There were two counselors who came to talk to me about treatment. I agreed with them but I couldn't even walk, so they held me up for three hundred feet as I feebly walked to the center.

Finding God and Letting Go

I was in the center for about three weeks when one night I started to cry and said, "God help, I can't do this anymore." The next day I felt like a hundred pound weight was lifted from me. I didn't tell anyone in the group therapy because it felt too personal. The old salesman in me would have blurted it out. Several days later a counselor asked the group if they noticed a change in me and most said they did. That's when I shared what I had experienced. It has now been thirty-five years since my last drink. It didn't happen by doing it alone. I had a lot of help; several care groups and very good, caring friends.

I am so grateful that I was sober for five years before my mother passed away. Towards the end of her life I was leaving her room at the nursing home and she said something that I'll never forget, "Bobby, you're ok now, aren't you?"

My dad committed suicide from alcoholism at the age of seventy. Only a few years before, my best friend had done the same thing in the camp next to my parents; although, depression was his reason. My father's friend also did the same because of alcohol and lived only two houses away. His wife came over and said she heard a loud noise and thought something may have happened to her husband. I went over and found him still alive after shooting himself in the solar plexus with a 16 gauge shot gun. Since both husband and wife were alcoholics, I wanted to make sure she hadn't shot him. I asked him why he did it, and he said, "That damn shot gun, how come I'm still alive?" A few moments later he died.

Golf

A few years ago I had my picture taken alongside my son-in-law Duffy, who has been my playing partner for nearly thirty years.

Three local papers did an article on me. I was 85 and had just finished playing my 1,000th hole on Sept. 18, 2012 for the year at Eagle Bluff Golf Club in Hurley, WI. What made this story unique is I had survived three major surgeries just in the previous few years. Is it any wonder why my friends call me Old Grateful Bob? The local PGA golf pro said it was quite an accomplishment for what I had been through. If only he knew more of what I have survived. I golfed 1000 holes the following year and I'm still golfing now at 89.

The ninth hole experience. It was uphill and one hundred thirty yards away. It had a two-tier green with the hole on the bottom tier so you shot blind. I made a beautiful swing and figured to be near the hole; possibly a hole-in-one! As I got to the green, the bartender was driving by. I couldn't find my ball, I even looked in the cup. The bartender happened to be driving by and asked if I was looking for my ball and I said, "Yes." She said, "A fox came by and ran off with it. Sorry to say but you were only two feet away from the hole." At that time, we had so many foxes at the course that we made national news with Dan Rather.

Surgeries

The first of these surgeries was quite eventful. It was 1995 and I was having open heart triple bypass surgery. When they hit me with the paddles to restart my heart, I came out of the anesthetic. My chest was wide open and I remember trying to yell or raise my arms but couldn't because they administered a drug to prevent any movement. I was mumbling afterwards in intensive care where the anesthesiologist was and she mentioned being aware that something had happened. I had nightmares for months. Around this time, 20/20 and Tom Brokaw were talking about other people having this happen to them. My daughter said I should write a book. One interesting fact: the surgeon told me that he couldn't do anything for part of my heart but he could buy me three to four more years of life. That was 1995, it's now 2016.

The second major surgery was done after I had done a urine test at the V.A. clinic and it showed blood. While there, they had me go for an ultrasound at 7:30 in the morning. I was about twenty-five miles from home when the clinic called me on my cell phone and told me I had a large aneurysm that could rupture. I was advised to head to the hospital where an ambulance was waiting to take me to Green Bay, WI where I would have family to take care of me after the surgery. Boy, this brought back memories from my childhood about my brother. This is exactly what he died from when he was only thirteen years old.

They stuck a tube in my main aorta and proceeded with the operation. At this same time, I had shingles which made the operation even more at risk for infection, but they went ahead because it could rupture at any time. After only four days I left the hospital. I was seventy-eight years old at the time. The doctor asked what do they make you Finlanders out of and I said we call it SISU. Finlander fortitude.

The final surgery (fingers crossed) was done when I was eighty-three. It was open heart surgery again. The doctor said it would be risky because he would follow the old scar tissue; the scalpel could slip and nick my heart. Before the surgery, I had to have oral surgery to have five molars and the jawbone removed so there wouldn't be any infection from those either. I had been taking the blood thinner Cummadin for seventeen years. My whole jaw and throat area turned to the color black! Boy did I get scared looks when I was in public. Anyhow, the doctor installed a pig's valve and the surgery went on without a hitch. After explaining to this doctor what SISU was all about, I walked out after only three days. He wanted me to stay and show the forty somethings that older men could walk the next day after surgery.

Is it any wonder why I call myself Old Grateful Bob?

Recovery

Hopefully you have enjoyed reading my story. I would like to leave you with this advice: until I found my bottom and reached the point that I had had enough, I could not arrive at sobriety. Boy, I wish I had listened to this many years ago. This is meant for any addiction. Psssttt…. I advise not to "keep digging."

Sincerely,

Ol' Grateful Bob Nylund

Made in the USA
Middletown, DE
29 December 2021

57212769R00027